How To Find Your Soulmate

This Book Will Teach You How To Recognize Love When
You See It And How To Spot Relationship
Red Flags So That The Love Of Your Life May Not Be As
Far Away As You Think

Wade Arroyo

TABLE OF CONTENT

Introduction 1

How Do You Meet Him? 2

Letting Love In 12

What Message Does Your Physical Presentation Transmit About Your Identity? 30

Locating Suitable Male Individuals 51

Integrating Affectionate And Amorous Gestures To Foster A Deeper Connection With Your Partner 58

How To Engage In Meaningful Dialogue With Female Individuals 67

You Will Experience A Profound Sense Of Connection As Opposed To Merely Experiencing Mutual Attraction 76

Preparatory Measures To Undertake Prior To Commencing The Utilization Of The Law Of Attraction 95

How To Establish Healthy Boundaries: Recognize Your Personal Identity 113

Introduction

Your task is not to seek admiration, but rather to diligently identify and overcome any internal obstacles that have hindered its attainment.

Concerning the pursuit of observing affection, many of us experience a sense of powerlessness - as if it is entirely beyond our control. This should not insinuate any deficiency in the guidance we receive from well-prepared sources on how to find love, such as "putting oneself forward," "smiling at strangers," "trying out this dating platform," "having a trusted companion arrange a meeting," or "ceasing to date unsuitable individuals." While these suggestions are not without merit, they tend to only scratch the surface in terms of the ultimate objective of genuinely discovering love. Irrespective of the multitude of strategies we endeavor, we may still encounter the very obstacles that lead us to believe that perceiving affection is more reliant on fortuitousness rather than fortitude. Nevertheless, esteemed clinician and scientist Dr. Lisa Firestone presents a compelling perspective that there are unequivocal aspects within ourselves that we can effectively address. These endeavors not only lead us to the discovery of love but also aid in establishing a solid foundation for enduring and gratifying relationships. Dr. Firestone, a renowned author of Sex and Love in Intimate Relationships, boasts an extensive background of more than three decades working closely with couples, during which time he has extensively elaborated on the significance of deep emotional bonds. In this context, we have the opportunity to receive insights from her regarding the factors that hinder our ability to find love, as well as the most effective strategies for overcoming internal obstacles and attaining the romantic relationships we desire.

How Do You Meet Him?

This is unequivocally one of the inquiries and grievances frequently voiced by unmarried females: "In what locations can I encounter men of high caliber?"
While it is difficult to determine a universally optimal approach for finding a suitable partner, the most effective

method is the one that engenders a sense of personal ease. There exist numerous avenues through which one can acquaint oneself with gentlemen, including conventional offline methods, digitalized platforms for dating, speed dating events, and the possibility of engaging a dating agency. The final category is a subdivision within the realm of virtual dating, as it employs a digital database of individuals to facilitate customized matchmaking for couples.

I will provide assistance in navigating the most commonly favored options, namely the conventional and digital methods of dating. Regardless of the manner in which individuals come into contact, it is imperative to consistently adhere to the same guiding principles.

Traditional (Offline)

Suppose that you encounter an individual amidst a familial, societal, or leisurely engagement. In circumstances of this nature, one is able to observe his interactions with others. One can obtain an understanding of his conduct in the presence of others. Although this may only provide a limited glimpse into his character, it is possible to gradually form a preliminary understanding of his identity.

It would be advantageous to have an encounter with him amidst engaging in a regularly scheduled leisure pursuit. You must bear in mind that this is merely a minuscule representation of his character.

The advantage of encountering someone in such circumstances lies in the opportunity to observe and acquire knowledge without the burden of romantic involvement. This stage may aptly be referred to as the pre-dating phase. Exercise patience when encountering an individual of this nature. Prior to commencing a romantic relationship, it is advisable to inquire extensively and seek clarification on any uncertainties.

Please refer to the section titled "Inquiries to make before establishing an emotional connection with a man." It is imperative that your inquiries align with your desired attributes in a relationship and the specific traits you seek in a potential partner.

Please assess your criteria and ensure that he aligns with them.

Expanding one's social network by engaging with a variety of individuals is crucial, as it enables a person to broaden their social connections, rather than focusing solely on establishing a connection with a particular individual. One can never predict who might be able to identify the ideal partner for an individual. To foster a mindset of embracing new acquaintances and facilitating effortless interactions with a multitude of individuals, we provide you with a compilation of viable activities to consider:

Become a member of a social, cultural, or athletic organization.
Enroll in a course to acquire a new skill
Participate in a social group organized for individuals seeking companionship
Do volunteering
Go to conferences

Attend networking events
Attend philanthropic gatherings
Take the initiative to orchestrate your own gatherings
Go to museums
Go to libraries
Go to bookstores
Visit local coffee establishments
It is imperative to bear in mind that consistently presenting oneself in the most impeccable manner possible can significantly enhance the likelihood of encountering one's ideal life partner.

Online Dating

There is no definitive superior or inferior method for meeting people; however, it can be argued that the realm of online interactions affords individuals the opportunity to connect with a significantly broader array of individuals who would otherwise remain inaccessible through alternative means.

Should you opt to pursue this endeavor, there exists a method to enhance the probability of achieving favorable outcomes, enhancing the sense of security, and ultimately elevating your level of enjoyment.

With the gradual increase in the usage of dating sites, there is a simultaneous emergence of both unfavorable experiences and triumphs. In certain instances, women may experience a lack of ease or unease when engaging in online dating. They exhibit a reluctance to engage in the activity due to preconceived notions, or have previously attempted it to no avail.

Occasionally, individuals encountered highly unfavorable experiences via an online platform for matchmaking, consequently leading to a complete aversion towards it. Please take into account that dating sites can be regarded as platforms for introductions. Therefore, the actual commencement of dating ensues only upon meeting the individual physically, and up until that point, one can implement the subsequent measures in order to ensure a prosperous, secure, and enjoyable experience.

If you desire to avoid engaging in a long-distance relationship, it is advisable to seek opportunities to encounter individuals within your proximate geographical vicinity. Although it is indeed feasible to experience a successful long-distance dating or relationship, directing one's romantic interests towards individuals in proximity can facilitate the development of a potential relationship.

Be patient. There is a diverse array of individuals present on these platforms. Do not allow yourself to be disheartened by initial instances of unintelligent commentary or approaches. Moreover, it is highly likely that you will engage in numerous outings before encountering a compatible partner. Do not give up.

Kindly solicit additional photographs of him, and verify his presence on social media platforms. It is highly probable that he possesses a Facebook account, a LinkedIn profile, or a similar online networking presence. One could also conduct an online search using a search engine such as Google, thereby exploring photographs of the individual in question. Photographs have the ability to convey numerous narratives.

Ensure that you inquire about the appropriate matters prior to your encounter with him. Validate: Inquiries to Present to a Gentleman Prior to Commencing a Committed Partnership. His responses, demeanor, vocal inflection, and receptive nature can assist in determining if the individual merits your time and consideration. Engage in a telephonic conversation with him prior to your inaugural rendezvous. The choice of his words, the modulation of his voice, and his overall demeanor provide substantial insight into his character.

When initiating the initial encounters, arrange to meet him at a location familiar and comfortable to you. It is advisable to convene at a familiar café, restaurant, or bar. It is advisable to consistently arrange meetings with him in a location that is open to the general public.

In formal tone: "During initial encounters and early stages of dating, it is advisable to refrain from consuming any pre-served beverages at bars, cafes, or restaurants, should your acquaintance happen to have arrived prior to your arrival." It is the responsibility of the waiter to deliver your beverages. Never leave your drink unattended under any circumstances. Pay close attention to your instincts, and exercise a heightened level of caution during this type of gathering. You possess limited knowledge of the person's true identity.

An individual graciously shared with me the narrative of how she crossed paths with her significant other. She conveyed to me her trepidation towards engaging in relationships with individuals met through online dating platforms, expressing exhaustion at the lack of encounters with captivating individuals. She made the decision to undertake the endeavor and requested her friend to serve as her designated 'support person' in the event that she required assistance throughout the course of the engagement.

Thus, her companion arrived at the café prior to her. The acquaintance promptly identified the individual from the online dating platform and subsequently corresponded with the woman to furnish her with feedback. Consequently, the woman experienced a profound sense of empowerment and security, reassured by the proximity of her friend. The outing was enjoyable, and several months later, the three individuals reminisced and shared laughter over the anecdote.

The Significance of Your Digital Presence
Please ensure that your description remains concise and conveys a positive tone. In the realm of the internet, visual content reigns supreme. Your photographs will convey to him numerous narratives about you, such as your way of life and your sartorial inclinations, hence it would be wise to exercise caution in this regard.

Letting Love In

Having achieved a state of self-acceptance and proper self-care, you will now reflect a genuine sense of inner love to the world around you. The subsequent inquiry pertains to your capability to accept and embrace the affection that is forthcoming towards you and will encompass your presence.

Previously, my cognitive focus predominantly centered on the adverse aspects of my existence. For example, I observed instances in which my parents engaged in disagreements and preferred pursuing individual activities rather than going out together or enjoying outings as a couple. If inquired about the nature of my parents' relationship, my recollections are primarily dominated by the unfavorable aspects. To put it in another way, I previously had predominantly negative views on my parents' relationship until several years ago.

Upon altering my viewpoint and adopting a more optimistic outlook, I started perceiving the profoundly delightful nature of my parents' enduring marital union that has spanned a period of more than three decades. Their weekly tradition of embarking on joint bicycle rides to procure breakfast for our family on Sundays and their jovial pastime of engaging in karaoke sessions at home, punctuated by good-humored banter regarding their respective lackluster vocal abilities, revealed to me a charming and loving bond between them, which I had previously failed to recognize. Rather than interpreting such playful exchanges as instances of critique, I now perceive them as a source of amusement and shared affection.

My entire world changed as I began the awareness of looking for love instead of what I did not like. My parents remain unchanged in their current state. They have remained unchanged, as evidenced by their occasional disagreements, while I, on the other hand, have undergone a transformation by adopting a different lens through which I view situations and prioritizing positivity instead. I must say, it truly brought immense joy to my heart.

In the past, I have had former partners who exhibited a preference for pursuing individual interests and maintaining their autonomy rather than dedicating time to our relationship. Upon witnessing the love emanating from my parents and within our familial sphere, I encountered an ideal partner with whom we share a profound affection and delight in spending time together.

The change must first originate from you. By altering your perspective and cognitive processes, the events and circumstances encountered in your life undergo transformative shifts as well.

"Presented for contemplation are the following pair of inquiries:

1) How do you perceive the world and the individuals within your surroundings?

2) Do you perceive the splendors of existence, or do you primarily discern what you find displeasing?

The perception of the external world is a direct manifestation of our subjective internal state. Our circumstances are a reflection of our values and mindset, and we draw them towards us. By directing our attention towards the positive aspects, they will manifest themselves, whereas if we fixate on the negative elements and our undesirable desires, they will magnify and materialize as well. To accomplish this, it is necessary for us to conscientiously monitor our thoughts and the dialogues we engage in with others.

In recent times, I have received notable remarks regarding my consistently optimistic demeanor. Unbeknownst to them, my previous identity remains obscure. Upon reflection, my recollection of my former self consists solely of faint memories, with only vague details remaining in my recollection of my previous state. This occurs when you successfully relinquish all outdated beliefs and behaviors which no longer serve your best interests.

Once you have truly altered your mindset, perceiving the world with compassionate eyes, deliberately opting for a positive disposition, and consistently uplifting your own self-image and that of others through your words, it will not be long before you shed all remnants of your former self and emerge as an entirely renewed, dynamic individual.

Upon observing the abundance of love surrounding us, a corresponding increase in internal feelings of love shall ensue, thereby prompting a consequential revelation. You will be endeared by a larger number of individuals as well.

CHAPTER IX
Express Body Language

The conventional wisdom suggests that actions possess a greater resonance than words, and this notion particularly holds true in matters of expressing love.

Expressing one's love carries greater strength when accompanied by compelling emotions and physical gestures, compared to relying solely on verbal language. Because the utilization of body language is characterized by its sincerity and ability to evoke authentic sensations.

The importance of nonverbal communication cannot be overstated in cultivating emotional bonding. Engaging in behavior that mirrors their actions, sustaining eye contact, subtly leaning forward to demonstrate interest, and exhibiting a pleasant demeanor through smiling are several approaches to foster the establishment of that connection.

Furthermore, were you aware that the act of smiling not only enhances your physical appearance but also instills a heightened sense of self-assurance? A smile, additionally referred to as a contented facial expression, has been substantiated to have the ability to enhance one's physical appeal, as well as compensate for any perceived deficiencies in attractiveness.

CHAPTER THREE

Discovering Your Ideal Life Partner: A Guide for Finding True Love

The notion of discovering one's soulmate is a charming and relatable aspect of ordinary individuals' lives as well.

A soulmate is an individual with whom one shares a deep, profound connection, devoid of any sense of reliance or emotional neediness. The fundamental principle underlying a relationship between soulmates is the equitable fulfillment of needs, as a soulmate bond ought to motivate personal growth away from self-centeredness towards acts of selflessness.

It is the awareness that this individual, with whom you share your existence, is intrinsically connected to your very being. A soulmate is an individual who exerts a enduring impact on one's life. Your soulmate serves as your companion and fellow voyager on the ever-unfolding expedition of life.

Together, you support and aid each other in surpassing the limitations of your individual selves, facilitating spiritual growth and personal advancement."

Occasionally, the discovery of a perfect romantic partner is predicated upon fortuitous circumstances. Nevertheless, the prospect of encountering a life partner is enhanced through a shift in focus towards altering one's self-perception, as well as cultivating a more positive mindset towards love, dating, and establishing connections. Refrain from succumbing to the allure of relying solely on fate to find your soulmate; instead, focus on enhancing both yourself and your approach to dating in order to optimize the likelihood of encountering your beloved partner.

Section 1: Exploring Prospective Life Partners
1. Take pleasure in being unattached: Paradoxical as it may seem, it is imperative that you find contentment

and confidence in your single status before embarking on the quest to find your perfect partner. Extended durations of relationships can be attributed to the presence of robust physical and mental well-being, as well as a strong sense of self-assuredness exhibited by both individuals involved. In order to uncover your soulmate, it is imperative to possess self-awareness, clarity regarding your desires, and a sense of self-acceptance, all while aspiring for mutual attraction from an ideal partner. "Various strategies to enhance your solitary moments encompass:

Discovering captivating hobbies to engage in

Placing a high regard upon your interpersonal relationships and kinship bonds.

Engaging in a captivating and secure occupation

Engaging in exercises to enhance self-assurance and assertiveness.

Maintaining a journal can aid in maintaining focus and serve as a reminder of the progress you have made.

2. Develop appealing traits within oneself: Create a compiled inventory of qualities that one finds desirable in a life partner. Perchance, you may be attracted to a well-developed sense of wit or an enchanting smile. Perhaps you have a preference for individuals who possess a sporty inclination and actively participate in athletic endeavors. Alternatively, it is conceivable that you are inclined towards individuals with a fondness for literary pursuits. Irrespective of the attribute, endeavor to incorporate that quality within your own self. If you engage in self-improvement through these means, it is possible that you will eventually encounter an individual who possesses similar interests and goals. Furthermore, in the event that you do not encounter your compatible partner through this approach, you will still have enhanced your personal growth and acquired new skills.

3. Maintain a receptive perspective: Research indicates that individuals do not always possess the foresight to anticipate the characteristics that most captivate them. If one cultivates a roster of exemplary characteristics, it is highly likely that one will find oneself magnetically attracted to an individual in actuality who exhibits entirely dissimilar qualities. It is acceptable to establish a few non-negotiable aspects in relationships as you endeavor to find your ideal partner. However, it is advisable to rely more on your intuition rather than solely relying on a checklist of pros and cons. It is conceivable that you may find yourself astounded by the remarkable individual you encounter.

It is of utmost importance to mitigate psychological biases and preconceived notions. One should refrain from passing judgment on an individual solely on the basis of their skin color, religion, race, or age. Allocate sufficient time to acquaint oneself with the individual prior to establishing a judgement regarding the viability of a relationship.

4. Avoid individuals who are already involved: When you come across an admirable individual who is committed to another person, resist the temptation to engage in a romantic involvement with them. The majority of partnerships that commenced through an act of infidelity do not withstand the test of time. Their existence is rooted in a sense of scarcity and an intense yearning for what is unattainable, surpassing any genuine sense of dedication. It is advisable to exercise patience until your prospective partner becomes unattached for a period, in order to ascertain that your relationship stands a reasonable chance of success.

5. Expand your social circle: The greater the number of captivating individuals within your social network, the greater the likelihood of encountering fascinating individuals through mutual acquaintances. Broaden your social

circle in order to increase the range of potential romantic partners available to you. If you have the desire to meet new, promising individuals to embark on a romantic journey with, it is advisable to actively engage in the cultivation of friendships and establish meaningful acquaintances. There are several effective approaches to connect with individuals who share similar interests, which encompass:

Joining a meetup group
Participating in a hobby
Engaging in philanthropic work aligned with your personal values
Joining an alumni organization
Nurturing the relationships you have: extend invitations to friends for dining engagements, organize social gatherings, or plan occasional happy hours.

6. Maintain a friendly demeanor: By exuding a warm and approachable disposition, such as through smiling and laughter, you can promote a sense of ease and comfort among potential acquaintances. In order to promote a

sense of openness and encourage someone to share, it is advisable to maintain a receptive body posture and interact with them in a warm and approachable manner. Engaging in casual and lighthearted interaction with someone to whom you are attracted can serve as a valuable means of discerning their reciprocal level of interest.

7. Embrace the prospect of blind dates: Your acquaintances possess profound insight into your true essence and your favored preferences. Allow their instincts to serve as a guiding compass if they perceive that you may be compatible with an individual within their social circle. Not every blind date culminates in success, yet there are indeed instances where fruitful outcomes prevail. Do not isolate yourself from the opportunity to encounter diverse and captivating individuals.

8. Acquire knowledge on the art of flirting: Various manifestations of flirting exist. Nevertheless, as a general

observation, individuals who demonstrate courtesy, appreciation, expressiveness, and utilize positive non-verbal cues tend to be highly adept in the art of flirtation. Individuals who employ closed-off body language, engage in mocking behavior, or display self-deprecating tendencies while flirting are generally found to be less successful. Please direct your attention to the following attributes should you desire to engage in flirtatious behavior or possess the ability to discern flirtatious gestures in others:

Smiling and laughing
Concurring through physical or verbal affirmation
Continuing the discussion
Employing a posture characterized by a relaxed and receptive demeanor, with arms, legs, and palms uncrossed.
Sharing personal details
Making eye contact
Asking questions

9. Maintain integrity and an air of intrigue in your online dating profile:

Countless individuals have found their life partners through the realm of internet dating. Nevertheless, it can prove to be a challenging setting to oversee. According to user feedback, individuals experience improved outcomes when they opt for candid yet succinct descriptions in their dating profiles. Invoke an air of mystery when individuals peruse your profile: refrain from immediately revealing your intentions. Employ the use of dates as a means of fostering understanding and connection, rather than relying solely on the profile to carry the burden.

10. Encounter individuals in exhilarating environments: Individuals tend to exhibit greater interest in others when they experience heightened levels of stimulation. Individuals with heightened heart rate, perspiration, and intense emotions may exhibit increased responsiveness to sensations of sexual attraction and affinity. There are various delightful and stimulating situations in

which one could potentially encounter a prospective romantic partner.
The gym
High places
Horror flicks

11. Convince yourself that there does not exist a singular individual destined for you: In the hypothetical circumstance where only one person is meant to experience true love with another person, a mere one in ten thousand individuals would achieve such a profound connection throughout their lifetimes. It is widely acknowledged that this assertion is unfounded: individuals frequently experience the emotions of love and engage in gratifying romantic partnerships. Do not overly fixate on seeking the singular ideal match; rather, devote yourself to cultivating enduring, harmonious, and affectionate connections. Observe if your potential life partner can blossom in your presence rather than relying on serendipity to present you with the perfect individual. Numerous instances

of profound love transpire through an extended duration, evincing that individuals attain soulmate status following numerous years of mutual familiarity.

What Message Does Your Physical Presentation Transmit About Your Identity?

Each of us presents a portrayal of ourselves, and this portrayal invariably mirrors our thoughts and emotions towards life. Take into account the depiction of that universally-known individual with unsavory qualities present at the establishment commonly referred to as a bar. What mental image do you conjure when envisioning his unabashed attempts to flirt with you? It is possible that he is displaying an unctuous expression, exhibiting disheveled attire, clad in inexpensive garments, and emitting an overwhelming fragrance. His ability to engage in meaningful conversation is deficient, as he predominantly demonstrates an inclination toward presenting sexually suggestive pick-up lines.

He undeniably possesses a commanding presence, does he not? Nevertheless, this is the kind of image that repels the majority of women. Indeed, it can be confidently asserted that this unscrupulous individual holds little regard for the opinions of others.

Now that you have a clear mental image of that gentleman, take a moment to reflect upon the image that I, myself, project. What impact does my appearance have on the message I communicate to others? It is plausible that you may be taken aback by the extent to which your selection of attire, hairstyle, eyewear, dental condition, clothing, cosmetics, and the absence thereof, inadvertently discloses information about your personal identity. The revelation may be unsettling.

The "Indifferent" Attire
When one presents themselves poorly in public, it conveys a strong notion of

indifference. By neglecting to uphold a certain image, one inadvertently projects an image that signifies a lack of intention or purpose. The sentiment conveyed in this statement is typically that of indifference, often associated with individuals who are preoccupied with parental or professional responsibilities, or individuals who appear dissatisfied with the prospect of forming romantic relationships.

The inquiry at hand pertains to whether an individual who remains unmarried and desires companionship may unintentionally convey an indifferent attitude towards such matters. Please take note that the sentiment expressed in the "I don't care message" generally differs greatly from the defiant proclamation of "You cannot categorize me!" Goths, emos, punks, and individuals who embrace nonconformity demonstrate a keen sense of fashion and effectively express their sentiments through daring and extravagant styles.

However, individuals who possess an indifferent attitude are inclined to actively avoid attracting any form of attention towards themselves. They desire to appear ordinary and are averse to the responsibility of engaging in social interactions. Indeed, it is highly plausible that their communication could be interpreted as a manifestation of antipathy toward the addressee.

Does this inadvertently convey the same message to individuals you encounter?

What are some effective means of conveying a nonchalant attitude towards one's appearance? Presented herein are a set of relatively modest criteria...

• Discrepancy in colors

• Wearing pajamas or sleepwear while in a public setting.

• Fashion that has fallen out of popularity • Fashion that is no longer in vogue • Fashion that is outdated • Fashion that is no longer considered stylish • Fashion that has gone out of fashion

- Apparel exhibiting blemishes or damage

- An egregiously poor fashion choice (without any hint of irony...think blue sweatpants)

- Aged, creased, or tattered attire

Collaborate in your endeavors to provide assistance to others.

Directing attention towards individual sources of gratitude within a marriage constitutes a highly efficacious approach to fostering intimacy and maintaining a strong bond. Engaging in voluntary work for a cause, undertaking, or philanthropic pursuit that holds personal significance can help maintain a relationship's enchantment and freshness. Furthermore, it has the potential to expose you to fresh viewpoints, afford you the opportunity to collaborate in surmounting challenges, and equip you with novel means of communication.

Engaging in acts of altruism brings immense gratification and alleviates the burden of stress, concern, and melancholy. Individuals are inherently conditioned from infancy to exhibit a natural propensity for nurturance towards their fellow beings. The more you actively contribute, the greater the improvement you will experience both as an individual and as a collective entity.

Second tip: Employ effective communication methods to maintain regular contact.
An effective exchange of ideas is vital for fostering a strong and harmonious relationship. You experience a sense of emotional tranquility and satisfaction when establishing a robust and intimate bond with your partner. Periods of turmoil or strain have the propensity to starkly accentuate the schism among individuals when their ability to

efficaciously engage with one another ceases. Notwithstanding its apparent self-evidence, one can invariably procure a resolution to any quandaries at hand through the act of verbal articulation.

Do not leave your spouse in a state of uncertainty; communicate your needs to them.
Expressing one's needs in words can often prove to be a complex endeavor. One aspect to consider is that a significant number of individuals do not sufficiently contemplate the aspects they prioritize in a romantic partnership. Although you may possess knowledge of your needs, engaging in discussions about them can elicit feelings of exposure, humiliation, or vulnerability. Nevertheless, I would suggest contemplating the situation from the standpoint of your partner. Providing assistance and empathy to someone you hold dear is a source of joy, rather than a burden,

If you and your partner have established a longstanding relationship, it is reasonable to assume that they possess a considerable understanding of your desires and perspectives. Your associate, nonetheless, lacks the ability to discern thoughts. Whilst your spouse may possess certain notions, it is highly advisable to articulate your preferences with clarity in order to resolve any potential misinterpretations.

Your spouse may possess a certain perception, yet it may not align with your requirements. Furthermore, due to personal development, one's preferences and aspirations undergo a transformation such that what was deemed necessary and sought after, say five years prior, may vary at present. Consequently, it is essential to cultivate the habit of clearly articulating your needs to your spouse instead of harboring feelings of resentment, confusion, or anger due to their consistent failure to understand them.

Take note of your partner's nonverbal cues.

Implicit communication plays a significant role in conveying our intended message through unsaid words. Nonverbal cues, such as maintaining eye contact, modulating one's voice, adopting a specific posture, and employing gestures like hunching over, crossing arms, or engaging in hand-holding, significantly impart more information than verbal indications.

You will possess the ability to interpret your partner's nonverbal cues, commonly referred to as 'body language,' and consequently respond in a suitable manner. In order for a relationship to thrive, it is imperative for each party involved to exhibit awareness regarding both their own and their partner's nonverbal cues. The responses provided by your associate may not align with your own. As an illustration, one individual might perceive a warm embrace as an affectionate mode of interaction following a challenging day, whereas another individual might simply opt for a leisurely walk or serene conversation.

Furthermore, it is of utmost importance to ensure that your body language and verbal communication are congruent. If you claim to be "fine" by uttering "I'm OK," while gritting your teeth and averting your gaze, your physical demeanor will reveal otherwise. The presence of affirmative emotional signals within your relationship evokes sensations of love and satisfaction, which are reciprocated by your partner upon receiving such expressions from you. When one's interest in their own or their partner's emotions wanes, their relationship undergoes a decline and communication becomes arduous, particularly in times of pressure.

Dating a Politician
Being romantically involved with a politician is inherently fraught with controversy in every aspect. When

involved in a romantic relationship with a politician, engaging in discussions related to their profession becomes an inevitable occurrence. During such instances, it is advisable to assume a non-intrusive stance, as even casual interactions can become intricate when pursuing a romantic relationship with them. It would be advisable to refrain from becoming overly agitated about a contentious policy or legislation and to avoid immediately resorting to vehemently defending one's stance with impassioned arguments. This is due to the potential establishment of a discomfiting and undignified ambiance, which would significantly detract from your overall enjoyment of the occasion.

It is advisable to examine the landscape of public affairs, and should you observe your political counterpart becoming impassioned concerning a policy issue, discreetly shift the subject of conversation. From a genuine standpoint, there is a higher probability that your companion will exhibit caution beyond your own when it comes to steering clear of divisive political matters. If you observe him or her effectively mitigating these issues, take note and align your conversation accordingly.

When engaged in a relationship with a politician, it may be necessary to acknowledge and adhere to specific restrictions regarding personal mobility and encounters. As an example, your significant other may decline an invitation to go out on a date to a nightclub renowned for its lively atmosphere. Additionally, navigating public spaces may pose challenges in terms of personal freedom if one's partner is expected to maintain a certain image. Even during a romantic dinner in your company, your partner might remain ever vigilant, periodically checking their surroundings for potential journalists discreetly observing nearby.

Imposition of specific limitations on your personal life might pose a considerable weight unless you possess an inherent ability to adapt effortlessly to the demands presented by varying circumstances.

When you accompany your significant other to social outings, it is possible that individuals may identify them and express an interest in engaging in political discussions over the course of the meal. This course of action may lead to a negative impact on your potentially enchanting romantic evening with your companion, with limited scope for mitigation.

Simultaneously, it is the duty of a politician to aid their constituents in enhancing their lives and fostering a higher standard of living. A perpetual sense of serving the public, garnering media spotlight, and achieving financial prosperity is ever-present. These reasons ought to provide ample incentive for you to endure the minor inconveniences of being in a relationship with a politician.

Politicians effectively cultivate positive first impressions through their strong handshakes and well-groomed appearances. Politicians exhibit a demeanor of self-assurance. They epitomize the ideal companions for office parties and dinners where one introduces their parents.

Politicians possess various qualities that tend to be highly appealing and attract public interest. A few key attributes they often possess are outlined below:

1. Kindly extend a friendly gesture of a smile towards individuals.

They possess an amiable countenance that readily appeals to others. This approach consistently proves effective for them, as it fosters a sense of connection between them and the individual they are directing their smile towards. Consequently, when you next encounter your date, kindly present a smile. It will assuredly convey a heartfelt personal communication.

2. They make physical contact.

Have you observed their consistent adherence to the custom of handshaking? They also engage in the custom of shaking hands with children. It is possible that their rationale rests on the notion that physical contact with an individual facilitates the establishment of an emotional connection. Hence, make physical contact with him as and when it is suitable. Gently and sparingly make light contact with his forearm during conversation, being mindful not to overdo it, as excessive touching may be perceived as intrusive.

3. Engaging in formal greetings and polite conversation.

They utter certain personal expressions that captivate attention. Phrases such as "How are you?" It is delightful to make your acquaintance. The main idea is that direct communication, addressed specifically to the individual, has a profound impact on that person, and reputable relationship guidance suggests that in order to make a man develop romantic feelings towards you, it is crucial to engage in personal conversation with him. Politicians engage in this practice due to its efficacy. To successfully evoke his affection, maintain direct eye contact with a fervent intensity.

4. Enthusiasm

If you possess an inclination towards seeking recognition and prominence, you might discover a sense of exhilaration in accompanying a political figure. They tend to attract considerable media attention, which can evoke an exhilarating sensation similar to dating a celebrity. Furthermore, not only will you attain prominence on the covers of newspapers and magazines, but you may also be required to undertake extensive travel as your politician counterpart conducts visits to their electoral districts. You will undoubtedly partake in social gatherings and occasions, affording you the opportunity to interact with influential individuals and esteemed members of society.

5. Contacts are readily available.

If you possess a diligent work ethic and a strong drive for success, you have the opportunity to benefit from your partner's vast array of professional connections in both the business and political spheres. Their extensive familiarity with influential individuals in their respective regions is the underlying factor, as a significant portion of their responsibilities revolves around cultivating significant networking opportunities.

If you adhere to the principles governing the game, not only will you have the opportunity to secure profitable contracts, but you will also elevate your career to unprecedented heights. This pertains not only to achieving financial prosperity but also to fostering greater public engagement. Being romantically involved with a politician can potentially inspire and empower individuals to actively engage in matters concerning governmental policies and public affairs.

6. Be prepared to undergo scrutiny

When engaging in a romantic relationship with a politician, it is important to recognize the likelihood of being subjected to public scrutiny, necessitating preparedness to allow such scrutiny into your personal life. The media keenly track each move made by politicians, and typically their actions are closely monitored. Given that you are associated with a political figure, your personal life may become subject to intense scrutiny.

Photographers and members of the media may potentially be present in unconventional locations and during unexpected moments, aiming to capture photographs of you and your politician companion. Such instances may occur, for instance, when you are departing for a restaurant or when attending a movie screening. It is worth noting that any consumption or purchases, including personal indulgences, may potentially be documented by the media and subjected to public scrutiny and commentary. Frequently, seemingly trivial matters such as your choice of reading material or engagement in a specific recreational activity can subjectively be interpreted through a political lens. Every action you take while in public will be subject to careful examination.

7. Conflicting interests" "Incompatible interests" "Contradictory interests" "Conflicting concerns" "Divergent interests

In the event of divergent perspectives regarding politics and governance strategies, there is a possibility of encountering conflict with your partner's stance. With the exclusion of politics, supplementary matters such as concerns related to humanity, international affairs, or even sports are prone to becoming sources of conflict due to the influence of one's political inclinations on their perspectives.

Not all individuals possess a predisposition for adhering to a singular ideology or adopting a comprehensive set of beliefs and principles in every facet of their existence. It can be vexatious when one's existence is governed by a predetermined framework. Nonetheless, should you possess an independent disposition and find discomfort in adhering to the directives of others, engaging in a romantic relationship with a politician may present numerous challenges.

8. Confidence

Politicians possess a tendency towards dishonesty and frequently demonstrate a lack of commitment to their promises, thus endangering oneself by placing trust in them. Hence, it is advisable not to wholeheartedly trust all the pledges made by your Politician companion, as it is prudent to exercise caution when considering any assurances received from a politician with whom you are romantically involved. You are now more knowledgeable, particularly if you are dedicating valuable time to being in a relationship with a politician.

Locating Suitable Male Individuals

The likelihood of encountering the suitable man within a crowded club bustling with numerous women seeking to secure a desirable partner is rather slim. There are no inherent issues with the club scene, however, it is probable that numerous individuals present tonight may not represent the ideal candidates for you. The predicament you face arises from the fact that, when assuming such a position, you seldom have the opportunity to authentically reveal your true self to the gentleman, all while contending with numerous other women vying for attention. This is the reason why numerous young women develop feelings of insecurity and start modifying aspects of themselves in an attempt to capture the attention of the male counterpart. You are essentially placing yourself in a situation wherein the likelihood of achieving success is quite low, to say the least. Should you happen to encounter a gentleman, it becomes rather challenging to acquaint yourself with his true nature whilst he is already inebriated with an excessive quantity of alcoholic beverages.

The key to encountering a compatible partner lies in frequenting the social spaces that attract suitable individuals. When I refer to the appropriate individuals, I am specifically implying those who are best suited to fulfill your requirements. If you persist in frequenting clubs as a means of finding a suitable partner, be prepared to invest a considerable amount of your weekends in this endeavor. The crucial aspect is to refine the search by placing oneself in environments frequented by individuals of interest. As an illustration, if you possess a keen interest in automobiles, a local car show presents an opportune avenue to engage with a multitude of individuals who harbor a similar passion. There is no prerequisite requirement of owning a car to participate; instead, registering and attending the event allows for a pleasant opportunity to socialize and engage with the car enthusiasts showcasing their vehicles. One can never anticipate when an individual might be unattached, and engaging in a conversation regarding his '67 Camaro could potentially initiate the beginnings of a connection. It is possible that you will encounter a gentleman who is independently strolling through the fairgrounds, similar to yourself, and engage in a conversation regarding a specific car being exhibited.

It is possible that you display a greater inclination towards reading and knowledge accumulation rather than displaying a strong interest in automobiles. Proceed to your nearby bookstore or potentially attend a local convention. Attend a book signing event or visit a venue that hosts an evening dedicated to the recitation of poetry. Situate yourself in a position that promotes a sense of ease and contentment. The individuals who will encounter you evidently possess similar interests as yourself, thus providing a noteworthy foundation for initiating a friendship. While it may not be customary to encounter your ideal partner at the library, it is not uncommon for individuals to unexpectedly discover their life partner in the most unconventional of settings. One frequently encounters anecdotes regarding couples serendipitously crossing paths in various everyday settings, such as supermarkets, doctor's offices, and even courtrooms. Do not allow the geographical constraints to deter you from venturing out; instead, adopt an open mindset to explore the various opportunities available.

If you intend to interact with gentlemen in a more individualized setting, you might want to contemplate hosting a gathering at your residence and extending invitations to your acquaintances, encouraging them to bring along their own companions. One can never ascertain the number of acquaintances who have recently concluded a romantic partnership within their close-knit social circles. When you host a social gathering at your place, you offer your guests the opportunity to observe an aspect of your character that typically takes longer to reveal itself in the course of multiple encounters. They have the opportunity to observe the nature of your friendships, witness your independence and vibrant personality, and ascertain your level of self-assurance and confidence. This approach provides an excellent opportunity to access avenues that may otherwise be closed to you. Please inform all of your female acquaintances that you will be hosting an event, at which they are welcome to invite any number of male companions they choose. By adhering to this practice, you can rest assured that every individual present at the gathering is a trusted acquaintance, minimizing any apprehension regarding unfamiliar guests in your residence.

The crucial factor in encountering the appropriate gentleman lies in positioning oneself in situations where the need for extensive effort is alleviated. If you exclusively engage in activities that genuinely resonate with your interests and passions, you will naturally feel more at ease and in alignment with your true self, and this authenticity will not go unnoticed by others. By surrounding yourself with endeavors that ignite your passion, you will effortlessly establish a strong initial connection with individuals who harbor comparable interests, ensuring a propitious commencement. If your town is hosting a wine-tasting event and you possess an affinity for various wines, positioning yourself in the proximity of individuals who share a profound fondness for wine will be opportune. By actively immersing yourself in these distinctive circumstances, you enhance the probability of encountering a gentleman who shares similar interests. By adopting this approach, you can refrain from feigning interest in something merely for the sake of the individual. Instead, you demonstrate your genuine engagement, which may prompt him to develop a desire to further acquaint himself with you. Upon strategically enhancing your chances and establishing a connection with a suitable partner, it is imperative to possess the knowledge and skills required to maintain and sustain this bond.

Integrating Affectionate And Amorous Gestures To Foster A Deeper Connection With Your Partner

Expressions of love can transcend mere verbal communication, as a romantic gesture holds the power to convey sentiments that exceed the three words 'I love you.' To foster a deeper emotional bond with your partner through affectionate physical contact, consider implementing the following approaches.

Physical affection and openly affectionate gestures play a crucial role in a romantic partnership, particularly in the initial stages. As a result, couples who are on their honeymoon frequently encounter challenges in refraining from physical affection.

In addition, they engage in moments of affectionate intimacy both in private settings and public environments, thereby distinguishing themselves from individuals in established long-term partnerships.

Ultimately, a mature form of love will mitigate the enchanting phase of infatuation. In the case of numerous couples, the mutual exchanges of intimate physical contact that previously served as initiators of sexual activity have become obsolete.

The significance of affectionate and tender acts within interpersonal relationships.

It is a widespread occurrence for individuals to transition briskly from one stage to another in a relationship. It is conceivable that infatuation has the potential to transition into a deep and sustainable love with the passage of time, thereby resulting in contentment for all parties involved. However, transitioning from one phase of love to the next is not as straightforward as one might assume.

Affection may occasionally emanate a brilliant luminescence, while on other occasions, it dissipates into obscurity. And this is solely due to our oversight of the glaring and essential components that contribute to a prosperous and fulfilling partnership.

As a relationship progresses, it is imperative that a suitable level of intimacy and physical contact is established. However, in addition to that, it also necessitates a significant amount of affectionate, tender, and platonic touches.

The intensity of physical contact and one's psychological condition

When two individuals experience profound affection for one another, verbal communication assumes a diminished significance. The pair will commence conversing in a novel language of their own creation, which remains incomprehensible to all others. Couples engage in communication through physical contact.

In complete candor, a mere touch has a greater impact than a verbal expression of affection.

Have you ever felt the desire to engage in an affectionate embrace or indulge in a period of comforting closeness with your significant other, devoid of any specific rationale? Have you ever felt the desire to seek solace in the warm embrace of your beloved and find comfort in their arms, especially during moments of melancholy and distress? Do you consistently experience a renewed sense of energy whenever you engage in this activity?

Intimacy and revitalization are rejuvenated within a relationship through the expression of physical affection and the embrace of close proximity. However, fervent and affectionate gestures uphold a relationship by consistently fulfilling our innate desire for love and nurturing.

Get Enough Sleep

Do you get nightmares? If you have recently endured sexual abuse or undergone a significant traumatic event, it is possible that you may experience distressing dreams involving being pursued, consumed, or descending from the sky. In due course, you will envision a scenario wherein you are confronting and triumphing over your assailant in a dream. I have effectively vented my anger through those dreams. Don't worry. You are not someone who takes the life of others. This phenomenon can be attributed to your subconscious mind seeking resolution in the realm of dreams. This signifies that you are undergoing a process of recovery. In the event that you experience distressing dreams, it would be beneficial to affirm to yourself that it is permissible to assertively confront these nightmares within the realm of your dreams before you initiate the process of falling asleep. It is crucial to bear in mind that dreams are constructed by the subconscious mind, which holds a fondness for suggestions.

An additional concern that hinders the attainment of a restful night's sleep is the presence of fear. It might prove to be quite arduous for you to retire to your bed. During the evening hours, I experienced a heightened sense of vulnerability and prudently ensured the presence of knives and baseball bats strategically positioned throughout my residence as a proactive means of self-defense, should the need arise as it had before. I would suggest considering the purchase of an alarm system; however, in the event that it exceeds your budgetary constraints, it may be advisable to acquire a cost-effective motion detector from Radio Shack. Furthermore, it is advised to avoid residing on the ground level of an apartment complex or in an unsafe district. Contemplate the prospect of relocating or residing temporarily with an acquaintance. If you were to experience an assault in your residence, I strongly advise considering relocation. If the authorities at your residential complex exhibit resistance towards releasing you from the lease agreement, inform them that yourself and a collective of ten individuals in close proximity will engage in peaceful demonstrations outside the office specialized in subletting and tenancy matters. Inform the leasing office of your intention to distribute informational brochures to prospective tenants, highlighting the unfortunate incident of sexual assault that transpired within the premises of their complex, as well as the challenge you face in seeking an early lease termination. Kindly ascertain from local law enforcement authorities regarding the necessary permits and regulations. I can assure you that the apartment management will provide you with the necessary measures to terminate the lease agreement prior to engaging in picketing activities.

Implement precautionary measures that instill a sense of security within you, while also recognizing the necessity of relinquishing excessive self-protection in order to attain a restful evening. When one successfully confronts their fears and achieves a state of profound relaxation during the nocturnal hours, it signifies the commencement of their recovery process. This represents a crucial milestone in your recuperation. Presently, I slumber profoundly, without any difficulties. You, too, will experience this occurrence.

Have Fun

Devise enjoyable leisure pursuits for your own benefit. One activity that I particularly enjoyed was engaging in a relaxing bath. The tactile sensation of the water upon my skin facilitated a reconnect between myself and my physical being. Additionally, you can explore mindfulness practices such as meditation, indulge in the tranquility of a lighthearted film, or partake in the uplifting experience of singing a joyous melody. During a period of emotional distress over the dissolution of a romantic relationship, I would frequently resort to vocalizing the melody of the renowned composition, "Zip-a-Dee-Doo-Dah". I am firmly of the belief that it is unfeasible to shed tears whilst performing that frivolous melody. Obtain your eccentric melody and vocalize with conviction when you experience sorrow.

Upon observing the positive transformations in your physical well-being achieved through adhering to your comprehensive health regimen, the subsequent course of action entails attentively examining your cognitive processes. In the subsequent chapter, we shall ascertain whether your cognitions are beneficial or detrimental in the process of recovering from the trauma.

How To Engage In Meaningful Dialogue With Female Individuals

The ease or difficulty of engaging in a conversation is contingent upon the individuals who partake in it. If one party demonstrates a lack of interest or an inability to initiate questions organically, then the conversation will cease sooner than anticipated. The objective of engaging in conversation while seeking a compatible life partner is to familiarize oneself with women and gain an understanding of their preferences and aversions. Additionally, this approach serves as an effective means of establishing rapport and laying the groundwork for fostering a bond. Conversely, it is essential that the other individual be prepared to engage in dialogue in order for the discourse to yield optimal results.

On occasion, when the discourse proves stimulating and fruitful, women are prone to experience an immediate sense of connection, prompting them to readily divulge personal information and establish a deeper understanding of men. Certain women develop feelings for men with whom they have engaged in enriching and meaningful dialogue. It resembles having a companion with whom you may engage in open conversations on myriad subjects at any given moment. Some individuals develop a sense of ease and familiarity with others as a result of engaging in conversation. They can establish trust by engaging in conversation with individuals. The initiation of friendships, connections, and other interpersonal relationships often commences with a singular, time-honored exchange of conversation. What steps must an individual take in order to engage in a meaningful and productive conversation? Presented below are a few suggestions for actions you can undertake.

1.) Encourage them to share their narrative - pose open-ended inquiries rather than ones eliciting simple affirmations or negatives. Allow them the opportunity to elaborate on their responses, and as they are recounting their experiences, demonstrate active attentiveness and remain fully engaged in the present moment. Several individuals pose queries, yet upon the woman commencing her response, they concurrently divert their attention towards their mobile devices or engage in alternative tasks. Engaging in such behavior is highly uncivilized and tends to elicit strong disinterest from women due to the offensive nature it embodies.

2.) Recount your narrative to them – discourse is a shared encounter. If individuals disclose their identity, it is appropriate to reciprocate by revealing one's own identity. There is no need to disclose everything at once. Reserve a portion for the following day, yet it is necessary to provide them with a certain amount. Inform them of who you are, and if your interest is genuine, this progression will occur organically.

Provide them with pertinent information regarding yourself such as your leisure activities, past experiences, professional background, areas of interest, and similar facets. Once you have adeptly introduced some information about yourself, the discourse is apt to seamlessly progress from one subject to another. Allow them to familiarize themselves with you to the same extent that you desire to acquaint yourself with them.

3.) Make necessary preparations - in order to prevent any moments of unease, it is recommended to conduct thorough research on the individual. Please exercise caution to avoid any behaviors that may be perceived as intrusive or stalking-like. Engage in this activity with the intention of gaining further insights about them beforehand in order to circumvent potential challenges. You may consider exploring their social media profiles on platforms such as Facebook, Twitter, Instagram, and similar platforms. Merely by perusing these accounts, one can glean insights into their true nature and discern their areas of interest.

4.) Endeavor to establish connections or establish correlations to the greatest extent possible – this does not constitute deviating from one's authentic self. This entails investing a small measure of effort to facilitate the progression of the conversation. If one is inclined to engage in a dispute with a statement made by a woman, it is important to consider that such a course of action may result in the termination of the conversation. Determine the reasons behind their beliefs and the rationale informing their perspective. This method also serves as an effective means of familiarizing oneself with another individual. Couples do not possess complete alignment in their beliefs. They exhibit discrepancies due to their status as distinct individuals notwithstanding their involvement in a relationship. They possess the ability to ensure that it does not impede their relationship.

5.) Pay attention – although this may have been reiterated countless times, it can often be the most challenging action to undertake. It is imperative to give attentive consideration to the speaker during their discourse. Active listening includes the acquisition of knowledge about the individual. Acquiring information that could prove useful in future circumstances. A woman may inform you of her ice cream allergy and you decided to display kindness by offering her ice cream on a particular occasion. It will be evident to her that you failed to give adequate attention and displayed a lack of interest in her discourse. You will incur a significant deduction of points due to this action.

When engaging in conversation with a woman with the purpose of acquainting oneself, make a genuine effort to develop a comprehensive understanding of her. Pay close attention to her and assimilate all of the information she is about to convey. This will enable you to assess your compatibility with her and determine the potential for a deeper connection. Active listening is of equal significance as well. You have the ability to engage in actions such as nodding your head whilst she is speaking. This provides her with the assurance that you are genuinely attentive and fully present. One may demonstrate acknowledgement or employ non-verbal cues to furthermore convey their engagement with her.

6.) Acquire the knowledge of appropriate inquiries – in the event of this being your initial interaction with her, pose queries regarding her interests and pastimes. It is considered inappropriate to inquire about personal or private matters during the initial encounter with her. This behavior is highly off-putting and runs counter to the initial stages of getting acquainted and making a favorable impression. One has the ability to attract individuals of the female gender at any given moment, however, once one embarks on the quest to discover their life partner, the nature of the endeavor changes significantly. In order to ascertain compatibility, it is imperative that you establish a deep emotional connection with her, allowing you to gauge the alignment of your souls.

7.) Delve further - when a dialogue is progressing smoothly and organically, and this has occurred on multiple occasions. Subsequently, it would be acceptable to delve further into the discussion. Now, it is possible to familiarize oneself with their apprehensions, capabilities, and vulnerabilities. This entails delving into a more profound understanding of the individual. You are not merely acquainted with her superficially, but rather, you are currently being exposed to her authentic self. Once more, respond in kind and disclose something about yourself at a similar level. It is crucial to bear in mind that effective conversations necessitate a mutual exchange wherein both individuals actively invest their efforts. This collaborative approach is pivotal to foster a successful outcome.

8.) Refrain from explicitly boasting about one's accomplishments; it is likely that such achievements are already well-known to the intended audience. In contrasting circumstances, refrain from flaunting it in their presence. Females have an aversion towards that. They would perceive you as being discourteous and haughty in demeanor. Allow the dialogue to convey your unique identity without explicitly proclaiming your exceptional qualities. You might not be inclined to engage in a romantic outing with a female individual who consistently extols her own beauty and remarkable qualities, would you? They share a similar sentiment as well.

9.) Avoid transitioning abruptly between different ideas, as it may give the impression that you are conducting an interview with the other individual. Once she has responded to a query, refrain from inquiring about a completely unrelated subject matter.

Inquire further regarding the same subject matter or provide your response subsequent to her. Engaging in a meaningful dialogue seems unattainable if your approach solely consists of incessant questioning. Allow her the opportunity to speak, and ensure that you engage in dialogue as well.

You Will Experience A Profound Sense Of Connection As Opposed To Merely Experiencing Mutual Attraction.

Jennifer, a middle-aged woman of 34 years, had reached the pinnacle of her emotional threshold. She expressed discontent with her interpersonal connections, holding the perception that each man she encountered possessed a singular focus on sexual pursuits. She arrived at the determination to cease her romantic involvement and redirect her focus towards her career. She uttered a final prayer before proceeding, beseeching the divine to bestow upon her a suitable life partner.

She perceives herself as a virtuous woman deserving of affection from an exemplary gentleman. She attended a networking event within a couple of days and encountered a pleasant, impeccably attired gentleman who perfectly matched her preferences, measuring approximately six feet and one inch in height, possessing a robust physique, and sporting a captivating smile. They engaged in dialogue and established a harmonious rapport during their time together.

Jennifer arrived back at her residence filled with joy as a result of the successful exchange of contact information. She was filled with intense joy, expressing gratitude to God, and holding firm conviction that he was the chosen one.

As time progressed, their relationship evolved from dating to a romantic connection. Throughout this period, she disclosed this matter to me and also discussed the prospect of it leading to matrimony. I experienced a sense of gratification for her, although an underlying intuition persisted that something was amiss. Upon further examination, it became apparent that, despite their amicable interactions, there was a noticeable absence of any genuine connection between them. They acknowledged and valued each other's contributions to the meal, but they did not derive pleasure from dining together simultaneously.

Please take a moment to ponder upon that.

They expressed satisfaction with the attention and superficial benefits of the relationship, however, beyond those, there is little else happening.

Regrettably, the romantic relationship proved to be fleeting and did not culminate in matrimony. He did not fit the criteria intended by the divine for her. The evidence lay in their dearth of authentic bond. In the absence of this essential quality, a relationship is unlikely to endure, thereby indicating that this individual may not be the suitable partner for you.

You will have the opportunity to encounter a myriad of captivating individuals, with whom you will engage in meaningful conversations and develop affinities. It is conceivable that one may harbor the belief of love towards a particular individual, an assertion which can indeed be accurate under certain circumstances. However, it is important to acknowledge that forming a profound and authentic bond with every individual is not an all-encompassing phenomenon.

While there may be occasional deviations from the norm, encountering such a connection on multiple occasions throughout one's lifetime is exceedingly uncommon.

It is a singular experience to establish an authentic bond with another individual. It appears as if two souls are acknowledging one another. This occurrence is not commonly experienced with the majority of individuals one encounter, hence making it a noteworthy criterion and essential foundation for identifying the individual designated by God as your partner - a distinctive and profound connection.

Chemistry vs. Connection

Do not conflate chemistry and connection.

Frequently, individuals assert to possess a "remarkable rapport" during our conversations. I shall inquire as to the intended connotation of this statement, and they will respond by positing that they possess congenial relations, share mutual preferences, or harbor synonymous interests and enthusiasms. Although this is truly remarkable, it does not necessarily indicate the presence of an authentic and profound connection.

Frequently, it is an integral aspect of a couple's compatibility.

To provide further elucidation, chemistry pertains to an individual's aptitude for harmonizing with others. It denotes a harmonious coexistence between two individuals. Chemistry serves as the foundation of a relationship, establishing the atmosphere for individuals to delve into a deeper connection, though this is not invariably the scenario. When two individuals cultivate a robust and authentic connection, they establish a bond. They derive pleasure from one another's company, irrespective of their mutual or identical pastimes. When a profound and genuine connection is established, a pair of individuals may find themselves at ease with being vulnerable. You acknowledge their imperfections and embrace the chance to spend time with them. Due to the presence of mutual acceptance, it becomes straightforward to ascertain one's identity in their company.

This is enormous.

You should prioritize establishing a connection that extends beyond mere compatibility and takes into account the long-term perspective. Chemistry can be misleading if one does not engage in extensive periods of meaningful companionship with another individual. This does not connote an obligation to coexist with someone; nevertheless, it is imperative to dedicate time to acquaint oneself with each other.

It is imperative that you engage in effective communication, express yourself openly, and divulge your deepest emotions. Without it, you will be unable to ascertain their identity. You possess a yearning to gain further insights into an individual, regardless of the fact that your understanding of their persona may not be exhaustive. Chemistry encompasses more than mere affability, companionship, or compatibility when it comes to interpersonal relationships. You aspire to progress, a circumstance contingent upon establishing a sincere bond.

Ultimately, it is imperative to differentiate between the notions of chemistry and connection. Therefore, may I inquire as to how one may ascertain the presence of such information? It is advisable to remain true to oneself.

Numerous individuals embark on dating, enter into relationships, and even enter matrimony while upholding a facade - presenting themselves as they believe they ought to be rather than who they truly are.

I have had the opportunity to interact with several women who have assumed a certain persona, conforming to societal expectations, irrespective of their personal comfort, driven by the belief that this is the sole means to attain the affections of their desired partner.

They managed to apprehend him with success.

They entered into matrimony, and in present times, they find themselves introspecting before the looking glass, pondering their identities, the turn of events, and the unfamiliarity of the person beside them.

When one is confronted by the harsh truth, it becomes evident that their marriage is in a state of ruin.

Avoid becoming entangled in the constraints of your personal expectations regarding the image you ought to project. It is acceptable if you find it necessary to undergo personal growth or improve specific elements of your being.

Embracing and authorizing this occurrence confers advantages upon you and your partnership. Nevertheless, if those elements fail to establish a genuine connection with your true essence, their endurance would be untenable, and ultimately, your authentic nature would be revealed.

Furthermore, it is important to avoid giving the impression that you derive pleasure from certain aspects of his character. It is commonly understood that refraining from engaging in sexual relations until marriage is considered ideal. Nonetheless, it is possible that a subset of individuals may have either deviated from or contemplated this expectation. This serves as an illustrative example, chosen for its profound influence on interpersonal relationships and marriages.

There exists an abundance of accounts featuring women who engage in amorous relationships with individuals of the male gender, only to experience a profound sense of discontentment, yet manifest a semblance of contentedness in their demeanor, all in pursuit of matrimony. You have retained or chosen to hold onto the belief that this is your desired outcome, hence you behave in a manner that suggests satisfaction with the sexual aspect, acceptance of his lengthy work schedule, and contentment with the limited time he allocates for you. You inevitably confront and manage all the undesirable aspects within the relationship, leading to a point where sustaining such efforts becomes increasingly difficult, resulting in an eventual explosive culmination.

This is an illustration of an absent connection. You expressed dissatisfaction with your current circumstances.

One feels comfortable in the presence of this individual when a rapport has been established. You have an affinity for them, you experience a sense of comfort in their presence, and you desire to spend time in their company. Despite their imperfections, you are content with them. You can freely express and candidly communicate your requirements to them. There is no justification for feigning authenticity when one already possesses a genuine relationship.

Everything is organic.

The importance of authenticity cannot be overstated, as it is through genuine self-expression that one is able to forge meaningful connections with others.

One must assert that a genuine bond cannot be established or severed, as I often opine. When individuals who have not encountered each other for a span of ten, twenty, or thirty years come together once again, it is as though the passage of time has made no impact, and former emotions resurface. Such genuine sensations are unattainable to manufacture or refute. You have the option to either feign chemistry and endure the behaviors, or engage directly with the individual. One may choose to disregard the matter and proceed, nevertheless, if the connection is lacking, it simply does not exist.

When one experiences intense fear of exposing vulnerability, it is possible for one to erect barriers and retreat, thereby inducing a comparable response in the male party involved. One could perceive the wall as a protective barrier, but the act of safeguarding one's heart pertains to shielding it from detrimental influences such as fear, anger, adverse energies, and various elements that might taint or obscure its purity, as explicated in the book "God Where Is My Boaz." That is the endeavor in which you seek to safeguard your heart.

One must refrain from entering potential relationships with their true identity concealed; otherwise, there is a high probability of undermining the relationship. You put at risk your capacity to embrace a potential meaningful bond with the gentleman who aligns with your ideals, all the while deceiving yourself into accepting the presence of an incompatible individual in your life.

How to Establish Effective Communication Once the Relationship Commences

After the completion of electronic correspondence and telephonic exchanges, followed by the inaugural meeting, individuals often find themselves experiencing feelings of apprehension. Communicating with individuals who are not visually present offers convenience, as it eliminates the assessment of one's appearance and reactions to the information conveyed by the other party. Nonetheless, acquainting oneself with an individual becomes more effortless subsequent to commencing a romantic relationship with said person.

Frequently, disillusionment ensues upon initial encounters, as the individual encountered in person rarely aligns with the preconceived notions formed from mere verbal exchanges. If you harbor concerns regarding this matter, I would recommend engaging in a Skype call, which would enable visual interaction with the individual. This will aid in alleviating any concerns you may have regarding the accuracy of the photograph they have shared on the internet. Naturally, you are welcome to request more current photographs when you commence correspondence; however, there is no substitute for seeing them displayed on the screen to alleviate any apprehension you may have.

After engaging in a series of telephonic conversations, text exchanges, and online dialogues, the subsequent progression typically entails arranging a meeting for coffee. The rationale behind this decision is that the scheduled meeting serves as an introductory evaluation of the candidate's potential to meet the desired criteria. The scheduled duration of the encounter is approximately 30-40 minutes in order to discern if the individual on the phone corresponds with their physical presence. Afterward, individuals typically proceed to a dinner outing either on the same night if they sense a positive connection or on a subsequent evening. It is customary and advisable to provide individuals with some positive reinforcement following a coffee meeting, indicating your interest in them and your desire to pursue further interactions.

There should not be a significant alteration once you meet in person. We do not expect you to divulge excessive personal information, therefore please refrain from discussing every aspect on the initial meeting. Nevertheless, it is crucial to maintain the fervor of affection by inquiring about one another's circumstances. A straightforward inquiry such as "How are you?" suffices to initiate dialogue, yet it is essential for both individuals to contemplate strategies for sustaining an engaging exchange and prevent it from becoming tedious. Demonstrate your active engagement by attentively listening to the discourse of the interlocutor and engaging them through inquisitive inquiries.

Gentlemen, seize this opportunity to demonstrate your exceptional leadership qualities to your accompanying companion. Demonstrate to her your exceptional poise and composure during the initial encounter. Poise and self-assurance are highly appealing qualities in a woman, and this presents an ideal occasion to showcase your strengths. After an extensive period of exchanging e-mails and engaging in phone dialogues, we have finally arrived at the occasion of our initial encounter. As such, it is imperative that we seize this moment and refrain from squandering this valuable opportunity. Extend a gesture of admiration towards her hair or her attire. Kindly convey to her that she possesses great beauty and express gratitude for the opportunity to finally make her acquaintance. However, it is crucial to exercise moderation in order to avoid giving the impression of insincerity. Please ensure that your compliment is sincere.

Ladies, seize this opportunity to carefully observe the individual with whom you have engaged in conversations over the past few weeks. Does he satisfy your expectations and correspond to the individual you anticipated encountering? Does he deviate slightly from the mental image you had formed? Demonstrate your curiosity by inquiring about his life and experiences. To make the most of each pause in conversation, it is advisable to share personal anecdotes that can serve as points of reference for him to guide the discussion during the entirety of your date.

If you desire him to discuss his professional life, engage in a brief discussion pertaining to your own. One can effectively shape his responses, consequently prolonging a productive discourse, by posing appropriate inquiries. Ensure that you do not leave him in suspense, but rather demonstrate your willingness to give this endeavor a chance. Additionally, it is appropriate to express admiration for his appearance, as it was the initial impression you formed when he approached you and escorted you to your table (if your initial encounter took place in a restaurant).

Preparatory Measures To Undertake Prior To Commencing The Utilization Of The Law Of Attraction

Upon completing the reading of the preceding three chapters, it is likely that you are filled with anticipation for commencing further. I certainly comprehend your viewpoint; however, embarking wholeheartedly at this juncture of the endeavor increases the likelihood of potential dissatisfaction. It is essential to attend to certain foundational aspects prior to embarking on the application of the law of attraction in the pursuit of an ideal companion. Please give careful consideration to the subsequent instructions. Prior to commencing, it is imperative that you clear these items from your path. When embarking on the application of the law of attraction, the initial step involves establishing a foundational structure. You will be unable to accomplish that unless you attend to these preliminary tasks.

Enhance your understanding of the constraining beliefs you hold

Constructing a brand new dwelling can prove to be an arduous endeavor when one elects to erect it upon unstable or loose underpinnings. It is imperative to ensure that you are constructing upon a stable foundation. The aforementioned principle stands true when it comes to your endeavors in utilizing the law of attraction. It is imperative that you cultivate an understanding of any restrictive convictions that you may be embracing. The challenge arises from the fact that, in many instances, one remains entirely oblivious to their existence. One might be unaware of their actions, yet they undoubtedly acknowledge the consequences they produce.

It is imperative to critically analyze one's behavior while attempting to establish connections with women and introspect about whether such conduct is influenced by personal beliefs. Do you believe that I am destined for failure, or do I maintain sufficiently elevated criteria when it comes to selecting potential partners? What are the factors that influence my behavior towards individuals of the opposite gender?"

Identify the underlying cause of the issue. In the majority of instances, much of it is determined by one's perspectives on other individuals, the concept of dating as a whole, one's self-perception, and the criteria for an exemplary partner. Ensure that these beliefs are beneficial to you rather than being detrimental. Additionally, ensure that the beliefs you hold are conducive to mobilizing and maintaining long-term action. In essence, develop an understanding of the beliefs that impede your potential for the type of success you would otherwise experience.

Eliminate or eradicate the constraining beliefs that are impeding your progress.

Regarding your limiting beliefs, you are essentially presented with two options: either eliminate them entirely or facilitate their transformation. Nowadays, a considerable number of individuals would inherently gravitate towards transformation. Indeed, our constraining convictions are inherent in our cognitive patterns. Modifying or altering habits can prove to be highly challenging. It is inherent for individuals to endeavor to reshape their restrictive beliefs. The issue lies in the fact that this transformation frequently leads to counterproductive outcomes. You tend to prioritize the attempt to rationalize your restrictive belief rather than effectively mitigating its impact. These entities are inherently distinct from one another.

When you eliminate your constraining beliefs, you eradicate their adverse effects. I cannot overstate the importance of this matter. Neutralization entails the dissolution of its adverse effects. It\\\'s still there. You continue to hold faith in those ideologies, yet they no longer impose upon you the compulsion to engage in adverse behavior. They are no longer initiating the negative impacts. This task is more challenging than commonly perceived. They hold the belief that simply altering their restrictive perspectives is all that's required, but in reality, they are effectively negotiating with these beliefs. They are merely attempting to give it a fresh coat of paint and presuming it to be wholly distinct. Do not succumb to that deceitful tactic.

Do not permit your mind to deceive you. Don't bargain with yourself. Don't justify your habits. Rather, direct your attention towards its consequences. Have you managed to modify your limiting beliefs, reconfigure them, or adjust them sufficiently to alter their impact? Redirect your focus towards the ultimate outcomes stemming from your restricting convictions, rather than dwelling on the specifics of said convictions. Regrettably, this situation presents a precarious path where it becomes all too tempting to cling to our current perspectives, often contorting ourselves in an attempt to rationalize our beliefs. Ultimately, despite all considerations, we invariably encounter the identical adverse consequences.

It is imperative that you maintain sufficient self-respect to refrain from engaging in such manipulative tactics. Overcome your constraining beliefs by transforming them to a degree where their detrimental effects are rendered inconsequential.

The alternative proposal, undoubtedly, presents a more direct approach. You merely dispose of them. In numerous instances, accomplishing this is indeed more feasible compared to the endeavor of neutralizing or transforming one's constraining beliefs. When one has made the decision to eliminate something, there exists truly no alternative. There is no necessity for rationalization. There is no requirement to provide justifications.

There is no necessity to exert oneself in assuming various comfortable cognitive stances solely to approach essentially identical convictions from alternative perspectives. You forego all such diversions and focus solely on securing victory.

However, as is evident, this task presents significant challenges. Regrettably, these are the sole options available to you. Many individuals are inclined to deceive themselves by entertaining the notion that alternative options or a hypothetical "middle ground" exist. Please refrain from engaging in such behavior. Pragmatically address and counteract or eliminate your constraining beliefs.

Find inner peace within yourself.

The essential point is to merely find ease and familiarity within one's own appearance. Please recognize that you possess an immense reservoir of untapped potential and possess the capability to manifest a reality that brings you genuine contentment. This endeavor demands a substantial investment of both energy and effort, yet it yields an equally substantial level of comfort. Given your understanding of your capacity to enact change, many of the circumstances that previously caused you distress will exert less influence over you going forward. I am referring, of course, to finding solace in accepting and embracing your past experiences.

We must acknowledge that the underlying reason for your perusal of this book lies in the fact that you have yet to encounter an individual in whom you have found the ideal match. It is highly likely that at some point in the past, you engaged in behavior that caused you to experience feelings of guilt. It is possible that you have committed certain errors for which you currently harbor repentance. Perhaps you have encountered a series of disappointments. Regardless of the circumstances, harboring feelings of guilt, remorse, and dissatisfaction regarding past events can have a detrimental impact. They constitute an impediment and it is unduly effortless for you to conceive an unfavorable cognitive representation, thereby impairing your ability to wield the faculty of imagination, creativity, and emotional impetus required to shape a fresh personal actuality.

What measures can one undertake to cultivate a sense of ease and acceptance towards one's personal history? Initially, it is imperative to address the matter. It is imperative that one directs their attention towards the matter at hand and critically assess the factual occurrences. The issue pertaining to previous trauma lies in our tendency to magnify circumstances with the passage of time.

The commonly held belief that "the passage of time has the ability to heal all wounds" is frequently proven incorrect.

Indeed, it is often the case that as we distance ourselves from the initial trauma or direct experience, the event gradually amplifies in our minds, taking on a greater magnitude and appearing increasingly menacing. The most unfavorable aspect of this situation lies in our tendency to dwell on a perceived past trauma or embellished past trauma, which in turn hinders our willingness to explore new possibilities or derive satisfaction from present opportunities. Talk about crazy. Talk about self-sabotage.

Regrettably, a considerable number of individuals partake in such conduct. The solution to escape from this predicament lies in addressing and confronting our past. What exactly happened? Are there alternative perspectives to consider regarding that particular set of information? Are there any specific texts that could facilitate the development of a perspective conducive to yielding more favorable outcomes in your immediate life circumstances? I am pleased to inform you that in the majority of instances, the response is affirmative. That's right. Irrespective of the tumultuous nature of the encounter and irrespective of the extent to which you may perceive yourself to have embarrassed, there exists an alternative means of deciphering past events that, at worst, mitigates their negative impact and, at best, facilitates your progress.

You must overcome the weight of your past. The underlying fact is that a previous misstep does not inevitably bind you to the disappointment of that past. One should always remember that what has occurred in the past is behind us. There is nothing within your capabilities to rectify the situation. If you do not possess a time-altering device at your disposal, it is imperative that you relinquish your attachment to the situation. It is imperative to address and reassess one's past circumstances, reframe them, and channel them towards personal growth rather than allowing them to incessantly burden one's present state.

Chapter 6: Simplified Approaches to Dating

When you encounter someone who captures your interest, develop a profound camaraderie and mutually decide to embark on a romantic outing, felicitations are in order! Every connection, whether it be among relatives, friends, or romantic partners, maintains equilibrium and harmony. There exists an equilibrium between the amount of time one is willing to allocate to another and the reciprocal amount they are inclined to dedicate in return. In the event that you find yourself consistently engaging in acts of kindness towards the individual, all whilst maintaining sincere intentions and vulnerability, it would be advisable to approach them directly and inquire about the extent to which they value the relationship, in parallel with your own sentiments. Do not hesitate to address this matter, as it is an endeavor in which you have put considerable effort. Hence, it is advisable to make earnest attempts to find a resolution. Delicately broach the subject, ensuring that they perceive your sincerity and gradually come to acknowledge their error. The initial stride towards fostering a remarkable relationship entails embracing openness. Nevertheless, within this particular section, I shall elucidate upon techniques to sustain and nurture the relationship beyond its foundational phase.

During the initial encounter, there is a tendency for an uneasiness and discomfort to arise as one finds themselves in the position of elucidating their personal background to an individual who is essentially an unfamiliar entity, considering that the aforementioned first date is typically conducted with a person of unfamiliarity. Despite the presence of a companion, one is embarking upon an uncharted territory, which may induce a certain degree of discomfort. In order to circumvent this predicament, it is advisable to simply embrace your authentic self. Alleviate the atmosphere by recounting amusing anecdotes that you have either heard or personally encountered. One could foster openness with them by reciprocating with an embarrassing personal anecdote in return for the sharing of one from them. It is indeed delightful when someone evokes laughter, thus perhaps you could aspire to achieve this as an objective during our encounter. In the course of your dialogue, it is advisable not to adopt an overly assertive stance in your quest for comprehensive knowledge about the other party. It is more appropriate to afford them the necessary space and time to share information at their own discretion. Furthermore, it is advised to refrain from excessive enthusiasm as it may convey a sense of restlessness. Following the initial encounter, the decision to pursue a subsequent date rests within your discretion. Exercise caution before hastily finalizing a decision, taking practical considerations into account, while also avoiding undue delay in reaching a resolution.

Upon embarking on a subsequent encounter following an initial date, one shall commence the process of genuine exploration and understanding of their romantic partner. With the accumulation of subsequent dates, the sentiments of endearment and allure are expected to flourish correspondingly.

Systematically explore each other's individual interests, engaging in novel and thrilling experiences to maintain the vitality and novelty of your relationship. However, avoid overly rigid planning and allow spontaneity to permeate your lives, fostering a sense of balance and contributing to the sustained fulfillment of a comprehensive partnership.

However, can one ascertain if someone harbors affection towards oneself? That individual will have a desire to maximize their time spent in your company. Authentic emotions will undoubtedly arise, yet refrain from placing sole reliance on your subjective sentiments. Inquire with your acquaintances about their perspective on the evident bond between yourself and the other individual. It becomes apparent through individuals' behaviors and verbal expressions when two individuals share a profound emotional commitment to each other. It is important to seek genuine indicators of a burgeoning relationship, rather than focusing on surface-level aspects. Exercising patience is crucial for maintaining a long-lasting relationship, as there will inevitably be instances that put your bond to the test, with the hope that it will ultimately endure such challenges. Maintain a receptive mindset and nurture the fervor and ardor within your relationship; exhibit a readiness to foster its longevity should it hold significant importance to you.

How can one ascertain whether or not they are not loved by another individual? Indeed, the individual in question will exhibit limited enthusiasm in engaging with you and display considerably less commitment towards the relationship compared to the level of dedication you exhibit towards them. Despite their pleasant words, it does not necessarily imply their genuine interest. It would signify that they possess a platonic relationship, typically devoid of any romantic involvement. When an individual elects not to continue and progress a relationship, they may choose to allocate their time elsewhere. Furthermore, they are reluctant to be perceived as 'being in a relationship' with you and will therefore maintain a secure separation and refrain from delving too deeply into that particular area.

Ultimately, allow it to occur organically. Love is an inherent inclination within humanity, hence discovering someone and proceeding with affection for them should seem innate. Regardless of any perceived inadequacies or a sense of being comparatively slower or less skilled, it is advisable not to be overly concerned, as each individual possesses their unique trajectory and approach towards forming connections with others. In the event of an unfavorable outcome, avoid excessive worry or distress. There are greater prospects that lie ahead in your life.

How To Establish Healthy Boundaries: Recognize Your Personal Identity.

Gaining awareness of your thoughts, needs, habits, preferences, values, and emotional responses engenders a greater understanding of your true self. Being aware of your own identity, desired personal growth, and establishing clear principles enables the establishment of mutually beneficial connections with others.

One can acquire the skills to effectively handle emotionally taxing and demanding circumstances by being cognizant of their presence. Grant yourself permission to release anything that is no longer of benefit or value to you.

The following are situations that can cause emotional exhaustion or intense stress:

Interacting with individuals who exude pessimistic vibes, display manipulative tendencies, make threats, engage in blame-shifting, exhibit bullying behaviors, or express anger.

Experiencing significant changes in life, such as the unfortunate loss of a dear one, the process of relocating to a different residence, the unfortunate occurrence of unemployment, or the unfortunate dissolution of a marriage, can result in having impractical expectations to fulfill someone's requirements.

Experiencing a sense of accountability towards the emotional well-being of others.

Holding the conviction that the conduct of others significantly impacts one's state of contentment

Due to a fear of love's loss, there exists some hesitation on your part to articulate your needs (potentially stemming from childhood experiences where non-conventional behavior was met with disapproval).

Experiencing a sense of responsibility towards the well-being and happiness of others.

Recognize your own proclivities.

Regrettably, the majority of individuals are subjected to the bondage of their established routines and behaviors. Over an extended period, it probably constituted the predominant narrative that permeated our existence. It gradually develops into a customary practice to behave in specific circumstances. In order to overcome a habit, it is necessary to develop an awareness of one's behavioral patterns and automatic reactions and consciously refrain from fueling them.

As a result of the Covid situation, my father has taken up residence in my home. Throughout his life, my Father has consistently displayed a discerning palate, gravitating towards meat-based or creamy dairy-based dishes that evoke memories from his early years. Nevertheless, looking at the recipes and photos that I have shared, it is clear that the meals I prepare are quite contrary to that perception.

Consequently, ever since relocating to this place, there has been a significant transformation in my father's dietary habits.

We tend to downplay the change and the fact that he has shed a few undesirable pounds through this dietary approach, yet there are instances where he does express discontent or voice objections towards the consumption of substantial amounts of vegetables. At that moment, a familiar pattern of behavior emerges within me, characterized by a strong inclination to appease him and a subsequent instinctive response of defensiveness, causing an palpable tension to permeate the space.

I acknowledged my responsibility in this situation and informed him that, although we would persist in maintaining a nutritious diet, it constituted a substantial alteration for him. We have come to the decision to either prepare a meal or arrange for its delivery on a weekly basis. If he were to exert his influence, he would refrain from making derogatory remarks about our meals. This mutually beneficial arrangement has provided him with a sense of anticipation while simultaneously aiding in the resolution of the issue.

This presented yet another opportunity for me to introspect and enhance my ability to react objectively, without allowing personal sensitivities to influence my response.

It is imperative to ascertain the underlying cause and individuals' respective contributions, including oneself, in order to address persistent problems and discern the recurring pattern. At this juncture, it is crucial to acquire the ability to "exercise self-awareness and prevent oneself from succumbing to setbacks." Then it is imperative that you grant yourself forgiveness.

Portia Nelson's autobiographical work, comprising five succinct paragraphs, readily comes to my recollection. Clarity will elude us until we gain awareness, assume responsibility, and make the deliberate choice to cultivate positive transformations, thereby liberating ourselves from our detrimental behavioral tendencies.

CHAPTER FOUR
Key learnings

In conclusion, the aforementioned are the most notable matters that have been addressed.

A relationship can establish a firm foundation only if one presents their authentic self while making a sincere effort to impress their partner.

One might need to diligently search amidst the wreckage in order to discover the invaluable gem of affection.

The fear of rejection can be daunting, but with courage, one can overcome it to find the love one desires. You possess the ability to regulate your emotions.

Efforts should be made to understand the interests and desires of the opposing party. This involves ensuring provision and safeguarding for his female counterpart. It is incumbent upon the woman to awaken this instinctive response.

Prior to fully comprehending love, it may be necessary to dismantle certain emotional barriers and engage in enjoyable activities; otherwise, you risk alienating those who hold affection for you.

Demonstrate self-respect and consideration towards others by setting attainable benchmarks, and observe how this amplifies the embers of affection.

If one is experiencing a sense of being unloved by those around them, it is plausible that self-love is considerably lacking. In the absence of self-adoration, one becomes incapable of reciprocating the affections bestowed by others.

What then?

There is no necessity for anyone to remain unmarried indefinitely. I trust that these suggestions will serve as a source of motivation for you to proactively engage with others and forge a meaningful connection with your desired companion.

Nevertheless, it is my staunch belief that a significant number of women fail to recognize a crucial element vital to achieving successful relationships:

Knowing how males think.

Encouraging an individual to express their genuine emotions may appear as an overwhelming endeavor. And this may significantly impede the establishment of a romantic connection.

Males possess a distinct perspective of the world compared to one's own.

Furthermore, this could pose a challenge in establishing a profound and intensified emotional bond, a yearning that men also experience on a profound level.

Through my past experiences, I have come to the realization that the essential element lacking in every relationship is not physical intimacy, effective communication, or romantic outings. All of these factors hold utmost importance, however, they seldom emerge as decisive elements influencing the success of a relationship.

A genuine understanding of the underlying factors that drive individuals is the essential element that is currently absent.

Concluding thoughts on the concept of soulmates

It is a worthwhile endeavor to relentlessly seek one's soulmate across the vast expanses of the earth. Please make sure that, upon arrival, you possess the same level of desirability to be pursued in reciprocation. The phenomenon of encountering two individuals who are impeccably compatible in all aspects is truly one of the most awe-inspiring wonders of the natural world.

The Red Flags

To be insincere would be to claim that no cause for concern arose during the course of our relationship. Subtle indicators, such as the manifestation of possessive conduct, began to arise, yet I persisted in my progression without attaining a definitive resolution. Have you ever disregarded warning signs that surfaced early on in your relationship? The majority of individuals, upon experiencing love, tend to perceive themselves as undefeatable. We believe that our affection possesses the strength to rectify any misfortunes. Nevertheless, not everyone has achieved an equal comprehension of love.

The most genuine manifestation of love possesses the transformative power to greatly impact society, yet only a handful of individuals possess the capacity to love in such a profound manner. In accordance with the verse from 1 Corinthians 13:4, it is stated that love exhibits qualities of patience and kindness. It neither harbors jealousy nor indulges in self-aggrandizement or arrogance." This is the divine interpretation of love provided by God, yet individuals have reshaped the concept of love to align with their personal encounters or lack thereof. To put it differently, certain individuals may define love as the assurance of financial stability, sexual compatibility, or the provision of a daily cooked meal.

My spouse had a contrasting encounter with love; his parents underwent a divorce. Contrastingly, my parents are currently in a state of matrimony. Our understanding and interpretation of love varied.

Despite the presence of love, one must never disregard warning signs. They act as an indicator along your expedition to decelerate and assess your prevailing circumstances.

I continued with my actions as a result of the belief that exerting significant affection towards him would elicit a transformation in him. I have acquired the understanding, nonetheless, that altering an individual's conduct is beyond one's capabilities, as it solely lies within the realm of divine intervention. Individuals undergo authentic transformation when they assume full responsibility for their conduct and exhibit a sincere desire for change. It is conceivable that change can be influenced by prayer, and it is to be considered that the power of God can aid in the process of transformation. This is not indicative of their inability or unwillingness to change, but rather stems from the fact that change cannot be guaranteed. Engaging in a relationship with an uncompromising stance, enforcing strict demands, or harboring unrealistic expectations regarding swift behavioral transformations is a recipe for calamity.

I strongly recommend that in the event you encounter an individual displaying deficiencies in certain aspects, prompt action should be taken to establish a comprehensive strategy outlining the precise steps that will be taken to effectively address the identified concerns. It is imperative to proceed further only once the situation has been sufficiently rectified. It is imperative that you either ascertain a genuine affection towards them and embrace their true essence, or refrain from pursuing a romantic relationship with them altogether.

CHAPTER EIGHT

Establish your criteria and communicate them promptly.

This chapter serves as the final section of this book, notable for its significant content. Failure to grasp this information accurately could potentially result in missing out on the opportunity to connect with your ideal life partner. Therefore, I strongly urge you to carefully read and promptly apply the insights conveyed herein.

Standards refer to a set of guidelines that shape one's character, encompassing both affirmative actions and instances of restraint.

Upon closer examination, the term "standards" can be deconstructed to reveal its root word, "stand". These guidelines are established to support you in maintaining your composure and avoiding mistakes.

It is advisable to establish personal criteria or benchmarks for evaluating potential partners. Failing to do so prior to the onset of a relationship and clearly communicating them in its early stages may lead to complications and discord. Establishing one's personal standards not only enhances individual worth, but also portrays a person of significant value. Modesty in one's behavior towards men is of utmost importance. Some women may not perceive any wrongdoing in sitting on a man's lap or affectionately referring to their male friends as 'sweetheart.' However, it is essential to acknowledge that such actions, albeit innocent in intention, might inadvertently convey misleading messages and yield unfavorable consequences.

Strolling during the late hours of the evening does not align with societal expectations of proper behavior; venturing out or engaging in social activities past 11pm, such as going on a date or receiving late-night phone calls, may project a perception of having lower standards or being easily accessible.

When you establish your criteria and encounter your ideal partner, it will serve as validation and indicate how they will comport themselves towards you.

Are you in search of a gentleman who will exhibit profound respect towards you, by graciously opening car doors and treating you in an esteemed manner? Establish your criteria and communicate them promptly.

When embarking on a romantic encounter, it is incumbent upon individuals to prioritize the development of meaningful connections and engaging in insightful conversations to foster a genuine understanding of one another, rather than viewing sexual intimacy as the ultimate objective. Observably, certain women engage in the act of going on a date and subsequently engaging in sexual intercourse within the same time frame. No, that price is far too inexpensive!

Establish a personal criterion whereby engaging in sexual activity is reserved strictly for after marriage, and maintain steadfast adherence to this guideline under any circumstances. This has proven to be immensely beneficial in my previous interpersonal connections. Whenever I contemplate embarking upon a new relationship, I conscientiously express my personal principle without delay, stating: "I hold profound affection for you and am desirous of entering into this partnership, albeit on the condition that I adhere to abstinence until the sacrament of matrimony has been solemnized." Indeed, I experienced a significant reduction in potential suitors, as it became evident that their primary objective was to engage in sexual relations with me, as indicated by their insistence on the inseparability of their desire for physical intimacy. Naturally, I held deep gratitude for their commitment to honesty, which in turn allowed for an amicable dissolution of our association, with each of us parting ways tranquilly. I also had individuals who purported their ability to achieve the task, yet as time progressed, they realized that I possessed a serious commitment to my goals, ultimately resulting in the termination of our alliance.

I encountered a situation involving an individual with whom I had a romantic involvement. We had mutually agreed upon abstaining from engaging in sexual activity until the occurrence of our wedding. He expressed his agreement with enthusiasm, seemingly deeply enamored with me. However, after six months elapsed in our relationship, fatigue took hold of him, leading to a noticeable alteration in his behavior towards me. On a particular occasion, an acquaintance of his contacted me, extending an invitation for me to visit his residence. Upon arrival, I encountered the individual in question in a state of distress, his eyes filled with tears, and donning attire reminiscent of mourning. Upon inquiring about his well-being, he remained unresponsive, prompting his acquaintance to elucidate the purpose of his call to me. He recounted that his acquaintance conveyed to him that we have abstained from engaging in sexual intercourse since the inception of our relationship. I affirmed this statement as it aligns with our mutual understanding. Furthermore, he elaborated that his companion has been enduring distress due to our lack of sexual intimacy, asserting that my actions are causing him torment. I smiled. This acquaintance of his humbly knelt before me for a span of one hour, fervently imploring me to engage in a sexual encounter with their companion. I firmly expressed to him that such a proposition would only cause him anguish and regret, as my decision remains unalterable.

I was required to articulate the potential consequences that could arise as a result of it. What would happen in the event of a pregnancy? As a first-time participant as well, I am committed to preserving my dignity during this experience, as it holds great significance as a gift to my future spouse.

A person who demonstrates an inability to fulfill my own requirements, is doubtful to adequately attend to those of an infant. Above all, it is an act of great dishonor towards God, particularly considering that I held the esteemed position of a chorister in the church, where I was widely recognized and admired. It is inconceivable for me to bring any form of disgrace upon God. I meticulously explained the situation to them and their response was met with silence, prompting my decision to depart, fully aware that it signaled the conclusion of our relationship. It perished through natural causes with minimal commotion.

Indeed, I experienced the dissolution of the relationship. I provided financial, intellectual, and spiritual support to this individual, yet bestowing my physical self proved to be unattainable. Under no circumstances was I ever intending to engage in such an action. Please be advised that merely observing others engaging in a particular behavior does not justify its adoption on your part.

Establishing clear expectations regarding punctuality in a romantic relationship can greatly facilitate your experience. It is imperative that you adopt the following principle: "Abstain from engaging in sexual activity until the sacred union of marriage has been established." This will serve as a protective barrier against numerous instances of emotional distress and disillusionment. Several individuals whom I had been involved with prior to marriage continue to maintain communication with me, with the exception of those individuals with whom I have lost contact due to my refusal to engage in blind infatuation. Instead, I approached love with a discerning mind and heightened awareness.

One should not hold the assumption that a Christian sibling possesses awareness of the moral implications of premarital intercourse, and therefore exercise restraint in openly expressing this standpoint. Hmm... you will undoubtedly be astounded.

From my perspective, I maintain the belief that if you possess genuine love for me, you would choose to retain my presence in your life, as I have an earnest desire to maintain your presence in mine.

Implement the principle of abstaining from sexual activity until marriage, irrespective of one's prior sexual experience, as this practice has the potential to elevate one's perceived value. This attribute possesses the potential to fulfill the criteria sought by your ideal partner.

In a realistic sense, achieving this may prove challenging, particularly if one has engaged in sexual activity previously. Nonetheless, if one does not create opportunities for it to occur, it will not transpire. For instance, engaging in clandestine rendezvous, frequently staying overnight in each other's residences, engaging in intimate displays of affection and courtship, (potentially escalating to excessive levels in the future.)

When engaging in a social outing with a gentleman, it is advisable to select a public venue, as secluded locations may present opportunities for engaging in undesirable behaviors (I acquired this insight through personal experience). If you are enticed by the gentleman's invitation to his residence, where he plans to cook a meal for you, and you possess reservations regarding his character, despite being convinced of his suitability, it would be prudent to proceed cautiously, particularly if you are compelled to attend alone. Please proceed towards public venues and engage in verbal communication in those settings. It is advisable not to venture to his residence unaccompanied should you desire to visit. Establish your criteria, articulate them promptly, and obtain confirmation prior to accepting and embarking upon the relationship. Establishing and clearly articulating your expectations and boundaries at the outset of a relationship is an infallible approach that safeguards against future complications.

Guidelines for Mitigating the Impact of Decision Fatigue

Allocate time for introspection and contemplate your errors.
Whether you ventured out without an umbrella and endured the consequences of being drenched while commuting to work, or you exceeded your budget due to an impulse purchase, it is advisable to take some time to reflect upon your mistakes.

Develop the practice of regularly examining your choices throughout the day. When your decisions do not yield favorable outcomes, it is important to reflect upon the factors that contributed to the undesirable result. Seek out the lessons that can be derived from every mistake you encounter.

Please ensure that you do not dwell excessively on your mistakes. Continuously emphasizing your mistakes can have negative implications on your mental health.

Limit the duration of your appearance - allocating perhaps 10 minutes per day should be adequate to facilitate introspection on how you can enhance your performance in the future. Subsequently, utilize the data you have obtained and direct your attention towards pursuing superior alternatives and making progress.

6 Recognize Your Shortcuts
Despite it being somewhat uncomfortable to admit, there is some bias evident on your part from time to time. Being objective is inconceivable.

Your cognitive faculties have developed cognitive shortcuts, commonly known as heuristics, which aid in expediting your decision-making process. Given the propensity of these cognitive shortcuts to impede one's ability to engage in deliberate decision-making over an extended period, they also possess the capacity to lead one astray.

One example is the utilization of the accessibility heuristic, which encompasses making immediate decisions based on readily available options in terms of models and data. If you regularly observe consecutive reports detailing incidents of house fires, it is likely that you will inaccurately assess the likelihood of encountering a house fire.

Alternatively, if you have recently acquired extensive knowledge regarding plane accidents, you may hold the belief that your likelihood of dying in a plane accident exceeds that of a car crash (despite statistical evidence suggesting otherwise).

Cultivate the practice of contemplating the cognitive shortcuts that result in detrimental decisions on a daily basis. Acknowledge the invalid conjectures that you may formulate regarding individuals or events and you may be able to render them somewhat more impartial.

Consider the Contrary

Once you have determined the validity of something, it is likely that you will adhere to that conviction. It is recognized as a psychological criterion termed unwavering determination. It requires substantial and irrefutable evidence to alter a conviction, surpassing the level of evidence that initially supported it. Consequently, there is a considerable likelihood that you have nurtured certain convictions that are not conducive to your well-being.

Take into consideration, as an example, the possibility that you currently possess limited aptitude in the realm of public speaking, hence, endeavoring to refrain from vociferating during communal occasions. Alternatively, it is possible to acknowledge one's deficiency in establishing connections, leading to the decision to abstain from pursuing romantic engagements.

You have also developed strong beliefs regarding certain factions. Perhaps you are inclined to agree with the statements, "Individuals who engage in extensive physical exercise exhibit narcissistic tendencies" or "Affluent individuals display unethical behavior."

The acceptance, albeit temporary, of convictions that are universally valid or completely accurate, has the potential to lead you astray. The most efficacious approach to confronting your convictions is by engaging with their opposite.

If you are convinced that it is inappropriate to vociferate in a social gathering, then systematically refute all the rationale supporting such behavior. Alternatively, if you are inclined to believe that affluent individuals possess negative qualities, please specify reasons as to why wealthy individuals may exhibit benevolence or show support.

Considering the opposing viewpoint will aid in dismantling unfounded beliefs, allowing for a fresh perspective on situations and the opportunity to respond with a different course of action.

8 Name Your Emotions

Individuals frequently express themselves using phrases such as "I have butterflies in my stomach" or "I had a sense of foreboding deep in my soul," rather than relying on emotive terms like miserable or anxious, to articulate their intense emotional states.

Many adults are simply reluctant to engage in discussions surrounding their emotions. Nevertheless, acknowledging your emotions can serve as a means of pursuing more advantageous decisions.

Your emotions play a pivotal role in shaping your decision-making process.

Extensive research consistently demonstrates that anxiety compels individuals to leave no room for chance. Furthermore, a sense of discomfort emanates from transitioning between different facets of an individual's life.

If you are experiencing anxiety regarding the mortgage application you have recently completed, you may feel hesitant to ask someone out on a date, as it may seem excessively risky to you.

Fervor, conversely, can lead to miscalculations regarding one's probability of achieving success. Even if the likelihood of success is minimal, individuals who anticipate potential benefits may encounter significant obstacles, which is often true in the context of gambling.

It is advisable to cultivate the habit of conveying your thoughts regularly. Please take note of whether you are experiencing feelings of distress, anger, embarrassment, unease, or disappointment. Take a moment to reflect on the implications of those emotions for your decision-making process.

Engage in soliloquy, treating yourself as a confidant
When faced with a challenging decision, consider the following prompt: "What advice would I offer to a close associate dealing with the same issue?" It is likely that by imagining yourself imparting wisdom to someone else, you will arrive at a more expedient resolution.

Engaging in soliloquy akin to an esteemed confidant diminishes some of the sentimentality inherent in the circumstances. It will aid you in gaining some distance from the decision and will provide you with an opportunity to be somewhat more impartial.

It will also aid in cultivating a greater sense of self-compassion. In instances when negative thoughts arise, such as 'This will never be successful,' you might instead choose to address yourself in a more benevolent manner. If you consistently fail to perform satisfactorily, there is a significant likelihood that your companion would not concur with that assessment. Perhaps you could provide something along the lines of, "You possess this." I am aware of your ability to accomplish this, if we were in discussion.

Developing a more compassionate internal dialogue requires consistent effort. Regardless, when you consistently cultivate self-compassion, you will experience an elevation in your cognitive capacities.

www.ingramcontent.com/pod-product-compliance
Lightning Source LLC
Chambersburg PA
CBHW050248120526
44590CB00016B/2258